MOTHER,

You Can Make It

FROM STRUGGLES TO BLESSINGS

FRANCETA SYMISTER LOPEZ

DAYELight
PUBLISHERS

ISBN: 978-1-953759-14-6

This book is dedicated to my mother, Angela Gowe, my rock; the strongest, most courageous, humble, compassionate, loving, caring, and faithful woman in this universe. God made just one of you, and I was granted the opportunity to be your daughter. I love you, mommy. Thank you for always believing in me, for pushing me to aim higher. Thank you for ringing in my head that I could still have a career. I remember you saying, "It's not too late; your dreams are still possible." Thank you for being a great blessing in my life.

Acknowledgment

I give all glory, honour, and thanks to God for the wisdom and knowledge to write this book. Without Him, this would not be possible.

Special thanks to my husband, Garnet Lopez, for his love, encouragement, and support.

Thanks to my children, Garnet Jr., Garet, Zachary, and Zaden, for keeping me inspired.

I also want to thank my publisher and her team, Miss Crystal Daye, for her advice and assistance. I am forever grateful. Thank you so much.

Table of Contents

Introduction

Facing a great ordeal can bring you to a breaking point, which can throw a person off course and cripple them in many aspects of their lives. How do you lift yourself from the valley to the mountain top? What is the first step to take in regaining control of your life?

Over the years, I have obtained a unique perspective and insights from my own life experiences, as well as other persons, which I will share in this book.

This book is based on a Biblical foundation. Its purpose is to restore heart, mind, body, and soul, which will propel the rebirth of dreams, hope, strength, faith, self-confidence, wisdom, and purpose.

This book is a guide to a purpose-filled life and a blessed future.

1

Give Your Struggles Over To God

We all face some things that cause us to loosen our grip on God and life. Our hope starts to diminish, causing our faith to waver. In that moment, as the struggle intensifies, we should look to the most high God and pour out our soul until our cry reaches heaven's throne. I know it is hard to pray during the toughest and darkest hour, but God has the power to turn your situation around. He can fix it. You do not need to do it alone. Turn it over to Jesus and let Him fight your battles. He is our present help in times of trouble.

God is our refuge and strength, a very present help in trouble. (Psalms 46:1).

Here are five reasons to pray during hardship:

1. Prayer is our defense against the attack of the enemy.

The devil wants to destroy you spiritually, physically, and emotionally. He can use anyone or anything to do his bidding, for example, family, in-laws, friends, church family, etc. When we do not pray, we become powerless, which opens up a loophole for the devil to step in; hence, bringing chaos into our lives.

Arm yourself with the Word of God and defend yourself with prayer.

For we do not wrestle against flesh and blood, but against the rulers, against the authorities, against the cosmic powers over this present darkness, against the spiritual forces of evil in the heavenly places. (Ephesians 6:12).

2. Prayer strengthens your inner man.

If you fail to build up your inner man, you will become spiritually weak; hence, having no strength to fight your battles.

And he told them a parable to the effect that they ought always to pray and not lose heart. (Luke 18:1).

3. Prayer gives you direct contact with God.

Talking with God daily helps develop a close relationship with Him. As you draw closer to God, He will meet you at the point of your need.

Draw near to God, and he will draw near to you. Cleanse your hands, you sinners, and purify your hearts, you double-minded. (James 4:8).

4. Prayer gives you peace of mind.

As you pray, there is this feeling of peace that fills your heart; there is a certainty and the assurance that God is taking care of all our worries and fixing all our problems.

The Lord is my shepherd; I shall not want. He makes me lie down in green pastures. He leads me beside still waters. (Psalms 23:1-2).

5. Prayer helps us to overcome temptation.

We are most vulnerable when going through hard times. The devil will send temptation your way. But as you pray, God will strengthen you and provide a way out.

And when he came to the place, he said to them, "Pray that you may not enter into temptation." (Luke 22:40).

Here are three steps to help remind you to pray:

1. Make a prayer timetable. You can paste it on your bedroom door or wherever you see fit.

When Daniel knew that the document had been signed, he went to his house where he had windows in his upper chamber open toward Jerusalem. He got down on his knees three times a day and prayed and gave thanks before his God, as he had done previously. (Daniel 6:10).

2. Set a schedule in your phone calendar with phrases such as "Time to pray" or "Let's pray." Ensure that it is set as an alarm reminder, so whether you are at work or home, you will remember to pray.

I desire then that in every place the men should pray, lifting holy hands without anger or quarreling. (1 Timothy 2:8).

3. Write little reminders on cartridge paper, for example, "Whisper a prayer today" "It's time to pray" "Let prayer become a habit." Then cut them out and paste them on your bathroom wall and anywhere else you desire.

Rejoice in hope, be patient in tribulation, be constant in prayer. (Romans 12:12).

2
Stop Feeling Sorry For Yourself

We all go through difficult circumstances, leading us to ask the question: "Why me, Lord?"

For me, it lasted for years. At one point, I began examining my own life. I also observed other people's lives, wondering how they could be so wicked, yet their lives were perfectly fine; no problems whatsoever. Unfortunately, life is unfair and awful things do happen to good people.

And we know that for those who love God all things work together for good, for those who are called according to his purpose. (Romans 8:28).

For about two years I wallowed in self-pity. I felt helpless. I could not help myself, my children, or my husband. The stares from people and their behaviors towards me just added to my predicament. Some persons were bold enough to make suggestions about what they think I should do to better provide for my kids. I felt powerless, useless, hopeless, and, most of all, helpless. I cried, I moped, but that did not change anything. I got up one morning and decided enough was enough. It was time to stop feeling sorry for myself.

Do not be anxious about anything, but in everything by prayer and supplication with thanksgiving let your requests be made known to God. (Philippians 4:6).

I prayed, then I took the first step to changing my future. I am my biggest fan, and that was okay. Jesus was my inspiration, and with Him, all things are possible.

I can do all things through him who strengthens me. (Philippians 4:13).

Here are four ways to eliminate self-pity:

1. Be thankful for all you have been blessed with.

There is always something to be thankful for. Believe it or not, there is someone out there praying for what you already have, so be thankful and give God the praise.

Giving thanks always and for everything to God the Father in the name of our Lord Jesus Christ. (Ephesians 5:20).

2. Help others.

You might be thinking, "How can I help others if I can't help myself?" Offer your service. Time is a wonderful
16

gift you can give. Volunteer at the nearest school or church. Helping others will also make you feel needed, which gives life more meaning. The bonus is that it also brings blessings into your life.

Give, and it will be given to you. Good measure, pressed down, shaken together, running over, will be put into your lap. For with the measure you use it will be measured back to you. (Luke 6:38).

3. Make a conscious decision to change what you do not like in your life.

Take the first step in changing your future; you can do this. Do not be afraid of failure because failure is a part of success. If you fail, try harder. God will help you.

Have I not commanded you? Be strong and courageous. Do not be frightened, and do not be dismayed, for the Lord your God is with you wherever you go. (Joshua 1:9).

4. Get inspired.

Draw inspiration from motivational speakers, books, the people you love, and, most of all, you can pull inspiration from God.

Fear not, for I am with you; be not dismayed, for I am your God; I will strengthen you, I will help you, I will uphold you with my righteous right hand. (Isaiah 41:10).

17

3
Unforgiveness

Being hurt by others can really hurt, especially when you hold on to it and refuse to forgive the people who hurt you. Unforgiveness is very dangerous. It can eat you alive. It plays upon your mind, drains your body, and if you allow it, will destroy your soul. Do not allow it to take over your life. Prolonged unforgiveness can cause stress, which can lead to serious health problems such as heart attack, high blood pressure, and mental health problems, including depression, anxiety, etc. God cares about your health. He also wants you to prosper. Let go of unforgiveness.

Beloved, I pray that all may go well with you and that you may be in good health, as it goes well with your soul. (3 John 1:2).

Six signs of unforgiveness:

- Bitterness
- Wrath
- Anger
- Clamour

- Evil speaking
- Malice

Let all bitterness and wrath and anger and clamor and slander be put away from you, along with all malice. Be kind to one another, tenderhearted, forgiving one another, as God in Christ forgave you. (Ephesians 4:31-32).

If you do not forgive, hell is your destination. The Bible states clearly that if you do not forgive, you will not be forgiven (See Matthew 6:15).

Think about it for a minute: you have been doing the work of God, winning souls for Christ, singing on the choir, etc., only to end up spending eternity in hell in torment all because of unforgiveness. Would it be worth it?

Please, my brother/sister, let it go. Forgive!

For if you forgive others their trespasses, your heavenly Father will also forgive you, but if you do not forgive others their trespasses, neither will your Father forgive your trespasses. (Matthew 6:14-15).

How do you forgive someone who chooses to hurt you? This can be done by following the example of Christ Jesus:

1. Make an excuse for those who hurt you.

Sometimes people hurt us unintentionally; they may say something to hurt our feelings unknowingly, sometimes they may even be influenced or pressured by others. Whatever the case, keeping an open mind can help us to forgive easier.

Jesus was being crucified, nails in His hands and feet, and blood running from His side. I am sure He was in excruciating pain, yet He cried out: "Father, forgive them, **THEY KNOW NOT WHAT THEY DO**." (Luke 23:34 – *emphasis mine*). I thought about this long and hard; how could He plead for these wicked people? Then God opened my eyes, and revelation came. I realized that they really did not know what they had done because those individuals were being manipulated by the devil. If we truly realize who our enemy is, we will forgive more quickly.

And Jesus said, "Father, forgive them, for they know not what they do." And they cast lots to divide his garments. (Luke 23:34).

2. Pray for those who hurt you.

The Bible tells us to pray for those who despitefully use and persecute us (See Matthew 5:44). Jesus prayed to the Father about the people who hurt Him. As you pray and ask God to remove the hurt and pain from your heart, Jesus will help you to forgive the person; hence, removing unforgiveness from your heart.

But I say to you, love your enemies and pray for those who persecute you. (Matthew 5:44).

Unforgiveness can block your blessings. Our prosperity is tied to our soul. In order for your soul to prosper and your blessings to flow, it is of utmost importance that you feed your spirit man. You do so by reading the Bible, praying, worshiping in songs, and fellowshipping in a church; hence, worshiping God with your whole heart and soul, in Spirit and truth. This is not possible if your heart is heavy with unforgiveness. Free yourself from unforgiveness so you will be able to worship God freely in Spirit and truth with ease, and as your praises go up, the blessings will surely come down.

Beloved, I pray that all may go well with you and that you may be in good health, as it goes well with your soul. (3 John 2).

4
Disobedience

S ometimes the suffering we go through is a direct result of our disobedience to God, which leads to many destruction in our lives.

But they did not obey or incline their ear, but walked in their own counsels and the stubbornness of their evil hearts, and went backward and not forward. (Jeremiah 7:24).

Two traits of disobedience are:

- Stubbornness
- Rebellion

Stubbornness is becoming unwilling, stuck in your own ways, and overshadowed by darkness.

They are darkened in their understanding, alienated from the life of God because of the ignorance that is in them, due to their hardness of heart. (Ephesians 4:18).

Rebellion is rejecting authority, responsibility, or disobeying rules.

For rebellion is as the sin of divination, and presumption is as iniquity and idolatry. Because you have rejected the word of the Lord, he has also rejected you from being king. (1 Samuel 15:23).

The consequence of disobedience and rebellion is clearly illustrated in the story of Jonah. Jonah was given an instruction from God: warn the people of Nineveh to turn from their wicked ways or they would perish. Instead of warning the people, Jonah fled because he thought they deserved to perish. Aren't you glad God's heart is not like a man? Jonah got into a ship heading in another direction, even though he knew what he was supposed to do. He refused and tried to run away. Jonah was sailing to Joppa instead of Nineveh. He was settled and asleep when the Lord sent a great storm to shake up Jonah. Jonah knew the storm was a reaction to what he had done, so he immediately asked the men on board to throw him off the ship. He was tossed off the ship and swallowed by a big fish.

Jonah's disobedience and rebellious behavior did not just affect his life but also others around him. His action endangered the lives of the others on the boat and almost caused a city to perish. His very salvation was also at risk.

Sometimes the storm we face is just a disciplinary action to get us back on track. Jesus loves us with an everlasting love, and He would never want to see any of His children perish. When He sees us heading down a path of destruction, He will give us a wakeup call to help steer us back on the right path.

Get right with God. Do not allow your neighbor to miss out on a life with Christ because of you; do not allow a community to perish because of you. Let your life model Christ.

For the Lord disciplines the one he loves, and chastises every son whom he receives. It is for discipline that you have to endure. God is treating you as sons. For what son is there whom his father does not discipline? If you are left without discipline, in which all have participated, then you are illegitimate children and not sons. Besides this, we have had earthly fathers who disciplined us and we respected them. Shall we not much more be subject to the Father of spirits and live? For they disciplined us for a short time as it seemed best to them, but he disciplines us for our good, that we may share his holiness. (Hebrews 12:6-10).

There are three paths that lead to destruction:

1. Dishonoring your parents.

I have had heated conversations with my parents, which I called "voicing my opinion." I should have kept quiet. We may not always understand a lot of the things our parents do, but we should exercise love, grace, and patience as God has extended to us. Never become ungrateful or forgetful of all the sacrifices they made for you, plus the honour that is given to parents is not based on their character or whether they deserve it or not. We should honour our parents because God said we should; that is it. Therefore, at no point is there any justification for criticizing, cussing, worst of all, hitting or fighting your parents. This path will only lead to destruction. Your life will be cut short. Death will be your reward. Let this never be your story, in Jesus' name! May the curse of dishonoring your parents be broken and the blessings of obeying and honoring your parents be fulfill as you walk in obedience, in Jesus' name.

Children, obey your parents in the Lord, for this is right. "Honor your father and mother" (this is the first commandment with a promise), "that it may go well with you and that you may live long in the land." (Ephesians 6:1-3).

2. Rejecting the good counsel of your pastor.

Pastors are there to guide us, so we should take heed to the advice, the warning, and the correction given to us with love. Ignoring the instruction or guidance given by your pastor is the reason for many downfalls and unfortunate situations we find ourselves in. I am sure a lot of persons can attest. Disobedience has led to so much of the difficulties we face. Let us correct our mistakes and start following the good counsel of the pastor God has set to watch for our souls.

Obey your leaders and submit to them, for they are keeping watch over your souls, as those who will have to give an account. Let them do this with joy and not with groaning, for that would be of no advantage to you. (Hebrews 13:17).

3. Turning a deaf ear to the voice of God.

If we are truly honest with ourselves, we would admit that there were times God spoke to us, and we told Him later, tomorrow, or we even ran away like Jonah. How long will you keep running from God? How long will you keep lying to yourself? You are delaying your own blessings, and causing yourself unnecessary troubles. What has God asked you to do? Obey the voice of God.

My sheep hear my voice, and I know them, and they follow me. I give them eternal life, and they will never perish, and no one will snatch them out of my hand. (John 10:27-28).

5
Make a Plan

In order to overcome difficulties, initiating a plan is necessary. Planning is deciding ahead of time what you want to do, which includes a specific goal to be achieved.

Here are five steps in creating an efficient plan:

1. Determine what you want to do.

Be specific about what you want to do. Pray about it, preferably before starting the project. Let God help you to make the right decision.

Commit your work to the Lord, and your plans will be established. (Proverbs 16:3).

2. Set a milestone.

Placing a milestone on your project or goal helps you to complete it at a certain time, whether it is three months, six months, or a year.

May he grant you your heart's desire and fulfill all your plans! (Psalms 20:4).

3. Put a time limit on everything.

It is particularly important to put a timeframe on everything. Without a time limit, you may never meet your deadline, and goals may never be achieved.

For everything there is a season, and a time for every matter under heaven. (Ecclesiastes 3:1).

4. Stick to your plan.

Carry through with your plan. Make little changes if necessary. Too many changes can throw you off course. Continue strong until you have reached your final goal.

But you, take courage! Do not let your hands be weak, for your work shall be rewarded. (2 Chronicles 15:7).

5. Never give up on your goals or dreams.

Circumstances arise at times, which may throw you off course. You may be unable to meet your deadline, complete a task, or reach a certain goal. If this happens, do not lose hope, do not quit, do not give up. Pray! Adjust your plans and continue working towards accomplishing your goals.

I can do all things through him who strengthens me. (Philippians 4:13).

6
Time Management

Managing your time is of utmost importance. The Bible tells us there is a time for everything (See Ecclesiastes 3:1). We all want to make the most out of the twenty-four hours in a day that God has blessed us with. Time management will allow you to utilize your time wisely in order to achieve a long- or short-term goal.

For everything there is a season, and a time for every matter under heaven. (Ecclesiastes 3:1).

Here are six tips on utilizing your time well:

1. Try to get at least eight hours of sleep.

Sleeping well is important. When you are tired, you will fall asleep in the middle of work. You are also distracted easily when you are tired.

2. Get rid of bad habits.

Bad habits hold you back. It prevents you from getting any work done, which delays your progress. The more time wasted is the further away you are from your dreams or goals. Get rid of distractions. Make a few changes, such as:

- Scheduling time to check social media and email.
- Turn off your phone notifications.
- Schedule television time.

3. Ensure you take break time.

If you are always working, you will eventually end up exhausted. Taking breaks prevents the body from getting burnout, which would result in time being lost that you do not want to lose.

4. It is okay to say no.

Your time is precious. Do not be afraid to say no. It is impossible to please everyone; therefore, do not waste your time on people or things that keep you away from accomplishing your goals.

5. Leisure activities.

Unwinding helps to relax the body, which helps the brain to function better. Also, spending time with family and friends can lift your spirit, which puts you in a good mood; hence, better vibes to work.

6. Focus.

The best way to achieve ultimate focus is learning to concentrate on one task at a time. Multitasking is a good skill, but it does not work for everything. It can leave you confused with a lot of incomplete task; hence, less work done.

7
Blocking Out Negativity

Our mind is powerful. It can either build us or break us. It all depends on what seeds we plant or allow others to plant. Whatever seed is planted will grow. Our minds are like fertile ground wherein it will process whatever you let seep through, so be very mindful of what you allow to take root; it will fill your mind-field. Therefore, if you allow negativity to take root in your mind, that is exactly what you will reap. Negativity can spread like wildfire, manipulating your thoughts and your every move, which prevents you from truly enjoying life to the fullest. It distracts from what really matters; therefore, stopping progress and eliminating your faith, hope, and dreams. It can destroy your future if you do not get rid of it.

Here are nine steps to help block out negativity:

1. Pray and bind every negativity.

When negative thoughts try to creep into your mind, or someone spoke a negative word over your life, pray about it, and bind it up, in the name of Jesus.

Truly, I say to you, whatever you bind on earth shall be bound in heaven, and whatever you loose on earth shall be loosed in heaven. (Matthew 18:18).

2. Change your mindset.

Try to see the good in every situation. Focusing on the brighter side will help to train your mind to think positively.

And we know that for those who love God all things work together for good, for those who are called according to his purpose. (Romans 8:28).

3. Love yourself.

Loving yourself will build self-confidence, which gives off positive energy. Love yourself for you are fearfully and wonderfully made by God. You are unique; every strawn of hair on your head is numbered. You are not a mistake. You are one of a kind. God made you special; He knew the world needed someone like you. Do not let anyone tell you otherwise. You deserve the best; give yourself the best, love yourself, and show yourself love because you deserve it. Do not forget that!

I praise you, for I am fearfully and wonderfully made. Wonderful are your works; my soul knows it very well. (Psalms 139:14).

Here are three ways you can show yourself love:

- Take care of yourself, for example, exercising, eating healthy, getting enough rest, and treating yourself.

- Have self-respect. Know your worth. Do not accept less than you deserve and do not depend on the approval of others in order to live your life.

- Forgive yourself. Beating yourself up over what went wrong will not change anything. We all make mistakes so forgive yourself, learn from it and move on. Life is hard enough without you being hard on yourself.

4. Love from a distance.

Sometimes to keep your sanity, your peace of mind and your salvation, it is better to love some people from a distance. It helps to establish a common ground. Sometimes space is all you need.

If possible, so far as it depends on you, live peaceably with all. (Romans 12:18).

5. Find your true calling.

Finding your purpose: what God intended for you to do, that is your true calling. Knowing what that is can alter the way you look at life because your passion has been awakened. It gives a certain drive, which places you in a good vibe; therefore, shifting your focus from negativity.

To one he gave five talents, to another two, to another one, to each according to his ability. Then he went away. (Matthew 25:15).

6. Be grateful.

There is always something to be thankful for. Being appreciative of all you have been blessed with brings about a sense of peace and joy.

The Lord is my strength and my shield; in him my heart trusts, and I am helped; my heart exults, and with my song I give thanks to him. (Psalms 28:7).

7. Surround yourself with positive people.

Some people are like leeches; they will suck the life out of you if given the opportunity. Who are you associating yourself with? Are they uplifting you? Think about it; do they even like or admire you? Watch for the signs. You can usually tell by the vibes a person gives off; there are clear signals of how they feel about you most of the time. So stay away from those people. Surround yourself with people who love you just the way you are, who support your dream and vision; people who celebrate you, and celebrate with you.

Whoever walks with the wise becomes wise, but the companion of fools will suffer harm. (Proverb 13:20).

8. Set an alarm reminder.

Setting a positive quote on your phone as a reminder can give you a boost of positive energy to carry you through your day.

For whatever was written in former days was written for our instruction, that through endurance and through the encouragement of the Scriptures we might have hope. (Romans 15:4).

9. Smile

Smiling is a wonderful antidote to brighten not just your day, but others around you.

8
Living Within Your Means

L iving within your means is basically accepting where you are now and not spending beyond what you can afford.

Precious treasure and oil are in a wise man's dwelling, but a foolish man devours it. (Proverbs 21:20).

Here are five ways to live within your means:

1. Create a budget.

Creating a budget will help to balance your expenses and income, which will help to stabilize your finances. Follow these guidelines to create an effective budget:

- Pencil out your expenses.

Write down all your expenses on paper and calculate the amount you spend fortnightly, monthly, etc.

- Cut back.

In cutting back, you need to differentiate between a want and a need. Make some sacrifices; let go of a couple of things you normally do; therefore, making some adjustments such as:

I. If you used to order pizza every Friday night, change that to once every month or two months.

II. Try cutting back on utility bills. For example, use less water by turning off pipes when not in use.

III. Unplug appliances when not in use.

IV. Buy energy-saving bulbs.

- Stick to your budget.

Sticking to your budget is not easy but remember the "big why": the main reason you are doing this. Think about the long term accomplishment that you will gain and let it give you the drive to be persistent in holding firm to your budget plan.

2. Avoid impulse spending.

Impulse spending is having the urge to buy something you do not necessarily need now. Try as much as possible to desist from doing this; it will only leave you with many wants and debts.

And when he had spent everything, a severe famine arose in that country, and he began to be in need. (Luke 15:14).

Here are three tips to avoid impulse spending:

- Take a shopping list with you when going to purchase items.

- Shop with a responsible person.

- Shop with the exact money.

- Avoid taking credit cards when going shopping.

3. Avoid taking out loans.

In today's society, we are deemed to believe we cannot live without loans, and it is our only source to survive in this economy with the cost of living at its peak, but it is a lie from the pit of hell. I have learned that it is possible to live without loans by saving towards what you want. It may take a longer time to achieve, but at least you will be debt-free.

The rich rules over the poor, and the borrower is the slave of the lender. (Proverbs 22:7).

If you already have a loan, here are a few tips on paying off your loans:

- Do not pay below your minimum.

- Double up on payment if you can.

- Do not miss any of your payment each week, month, etc. Missing will attract interest rates.

- Do a little hustling on the side to help pay off your loan more quickly.

4. Do not compare your life with others.

For some of us, it is our lifestyle that keeps us in poverty and prevents us from flourishing, stunting our blessings. Do not live to impress. If you do not have it, you just do not have it.

Do not be conformed to this world, but be transformed by the renewal of your mind, that by testing you may discern what is the will of God, what is good and acceptable and perfect. (Romans 12:2).

5. Save.

As Christians, all is given to us by God, including money. Money serves us; do not let it become a God in your life. Use it wisely to support yourself, your family, and persons in need. Jesus wants us to live an extraordinary life. Saving money prevents lack in your physical needs, which allows you to live a comfortable and luxurious life. It does not matter how small it is; "every mickle mek a muckle."

A slack hand causes poverty, but the hand of the diligent makes rich. He who gathers in summer is a prudent son, but he who sleeps in harvest is a son who brings shame. (Proverbs 10:4-5).

Here are four different methods you can use to save:

- **Get a "piggy bank."** This is a container that you can drop your coins in and save. Open it at six months or the end of the year.

- **Join a partner.** A partner is a partnership between a group of individuals who agree to save a sum of money, whether daily, weekly, fortnightly, or monthly. There is usually one established member who manages the partner; that person is called the banker.

- **Salary deduction.** This is done through the bank. You can make arrangements with the bank for a specific amount to be deducted from your salary.

- **Partner savings plan with the bank.** This method helps you to save towards a short term or long term goal through a monthly installment for a period of six months or a year.

9
Tithing

Tithing is a taboo subject for many. There are so many questions when it comes to tithing, but the Bible states it clearly that the tithe belongs to God, so do not be fooled into robbing God (See Malachi 3:8-9).

Every tithe of the land, whether of the seed of the land or of the fruit of the trees, is the Lord's; it is holy to the Lord. (Leviticus 27:30).

What is tithing? Tithing is ten percent of your increase.

You shall tithe all the yield of your seed that comes from the field year by year. (Deuteronomy 14:22).

Here are three reasons why it is important to tithe:

1. It prevents a curse.

When we do not tithe, we are robbing God, which will bring about a curse.

Will man rob God? Yet you are robbing me. But you say, 'How have we robbed you?' In your tithes and contributions. You are cursed with a curse, for you are robbing me, the whole nation of you. (Malachi 3:8-9).

2. You will be delivered from the devourer.

The devourer causes destruction in your life. He destroys all your livelihood and drains all your money, but as you give a tithe, the Lord will rebuke the devourer for your sake.

I will rebuke the devourer for you, so that it will not destroy the fruits of your soil, and your vine in the field shall not fail to bear, says the Lord of hosts. (Malachi 3:11).

Who is the devourer? The devourer is the devil; he will use every opportunity he gets to destroy your life. Do not be deceived; only God can slay him, and he promises to do so as we pay our tithe.

Be sober-minded; be watchful. Your adversary the devil prowls around like a roaring lion, seeking someone to devour. (1 Peter 5:8).

3. Blessings will overflow in your life.

As you pay your tithe, the Lord will bless you more than you can imagine.

Bring the full tithe into the storehouse, that there may be food in my house. And thereby put me to the test, says the Lord of hosts, if I will not open the windows of heaven for you and pour down for you a blessing until there is no more need. (Malachi 3:10).

10
Envision Walking in Your Blessings

When it comes to visualizing walking in your blessings, faith is the master key. It all comes down to faith, your faith. Look beyond the natural realm of your life and wrap yourself in the vision of what you are expecting to see. Hold firm to that vision, God's hand, and walk with full speed ahead.

He said to them, "Because of your little faith. For truly, I say to you, if you have faith like a grain of mustard seed, you will say to this mountain, 'Move from here to there,' and it will move, and nothing will be impossible for you." (Matthew 17:20).

What is faith? Faith is having complete trust and confidence in God, despite what is not seen.

Now faith is the assurance of things hoped for, the conviction of things not seen. (Hebrews 11:1).

Here are five steps in activating your faith:

1. Believe in yourself.

If you do not believe in yourself, you will never accomplish anything. All your hopes and dreams will wither away. Have confidence in God; believe that you are able to do anything because you serve a mighty God and all things are possible through him.

I can do all things through him who strengthens me. (Philippians 4:13).

2. Trust in God's Word against the odds.

When things do not make any sense, hold strong to God's Word undoubtingly.

Trust in the Lord with all your heart, and do not lean on your own understanding. (Proverbs 3:5).

3. Build your faith.

To build your faith, you must work at it, becoming more spiritual by praying in the Holy Ghost and speaking in tongues. This brings about spiritual growth; it builds your faith and as your faith grows, so does your strength and power; hence, walking in the authority given to you by God. Therefore, as you speak, every mountain, obstacle, hindering spirit will be gone, and blessings will be manifested fully.

But you, beloved, building yourselves up in your most holy faith and praying in the Holy Spirit. (Jude 1:20).

4. Listen to the Word of God.

By hearing the peaching and teaching of the gospel, then applying it practically to your life, this will definitely boost your faith.

So faith comes from hearing, and hearing through the word of Christ. (Romans 10:17).

5. Overcome fear.

Fear demolishes our faith. A faithless Christian is a useless Christian, and without faith, it is impossible to please God. Therefore, you need to conquer fear, and in order to do so, you must stay focused on God, on fire, and totally filled with the Word of God, which will increase your faith and fade away all our fears.

And without faith it is impossible to please him, for whoever would draw near to God must believe that he exists and that he rewards those who seek him. (Hebrews 11:6).

11
Hold On To God's Promises

T he only way to hold on to God's promises is to actually know God's promises. This means reading the Bible and studying the Word of God. God's promises were written to give assurance and build our faith.

It is so easy to lose focus in the midst of our situation, but as we channel our focus on God's promises, it will lift our eyes away from the present circumstances, knowing that God is bigger than any problem we face.

Let us hold fast the confession of our hope without wavering, for he who promised is faithful. (Hebrews 10:23).

Here are thirteen promises of God:

   1. He will strengthen you in times of weakness.

He gives power to the faint, and to him who has no might he increases strength. (Isaiah 40:29).

   2. He will never leave you nor forsake you.

It is the Lord who goes before you. He will be with you; he will not leave you or forsake you. Do not fear or be dismayed. (Deuteronomy 31:8).

3. You will never lack anything.

And God is able to make all grace abound to you, so that having all sufficiency in all things at all times, you may abound in every good work. (2 Corinthians 9:8).

4. Give your burdens to God, and He will give you rest.

Come to me, all who labor and are heavy laden, and I will give you rest. (Matthew 11:28).

5. Ask, and it will be given to you.

For everyone who asks receives, and the one who seeks finds, and to the one who knocks it will be opened. (Luke 11:10).

6. If you believe in God, you will not perish but be granted everlasting life.

For God so loved the world, that he gave his only Son, that whoever believes in him should not perish but have eternal life. (John 3:16).

7. If you confess your sin and believe in Jesus Christ, you will be saved.

Because, if you confess with your mouth that Jesus is Lord and believe in your heart that God raised him from the dead, you will be saved. For with the heart one believes and is justified, and with the mouth one confesses and is saved. (Romans 10:9-10).

8. God's plan is to give you a gracious life.

For I know the plans I have for you, declares the Lord, plans for welfare and not for evil, to give you a future and a hope. (Jeremiah 29:11).

9. God will deliver you from all troubles.

And call upon me in the day of trouble; I will deliver you, and you shall glorify me. (Psalms 50:15).

10. God will fight for you.

The Lord will fight for you, and you have only to be silent. (Exodus 14:14).

11. Every promise of God will come to pass; none will fail.

And now I am about to go the way of all the earth, and you know in your hearts and souls, all of you, that not one word has failed of all the good things that the Lord your God promised concerning you. All have come to pass for you; not one of them has failed. (Joshua 23:14).

12. God promises us sweet peace.

Peace I leave with you; my peace I give to you. Not as the world gives do I give to you. Let not your hearts be troubled, neither let them be afraid. (John 14:27).

13. A righteous man will obtain blessings.

The righteous shall inherit the land and dwell upon it forever. The mouth of the righteous utters wisdom, and his tongue speaks justice. The law of his God is in his heart; his steps do not slip. (Psalms 37:29-31).

12
Fight For Your Blessings

The story of Jabez is a wonderful example of fighting for your blessings and not giving up on your future. Jabez was a good man who had an unlikely past. Even his name was a daily reminder. He cried out to God, shamelessly pouring out all the hurt, pain, and all his fears. He pleaded with God to help him break the curse spoken over his life, which labeled him only to bring suffering to himself and others. That prayer changed his future. God granted his request and blessed him bountifully. His destiny was changed; his life was transformed. The lesson in this is: our past does not determine our future. Do not ever let your past hold you captive. Fight for your blessings.

Jabez was more honorable than his brothers; and his mother called his name Jabez, saying, "Because I bore him in pain." Jabez called upon the God of Israel, saying, "Oh that you would bless me and enlarge my border, and that your hand might be with me, and that you would keep me from harm so that it might not bring me pain!" And God granted what he asked. (1 Chronicles 4:9-10).

Why do we have to fight so hard for our blessings? All my life I had to fight for everything I wanted; nothing came easy for me. This always troubled me, but I realized that when the call of God on your life is not basic, your battles will not be either. The devil will stop at nothing to bring you down. Let that sink in! He will try every means to prevent you from fulfilling your purpose, calling, and destiny. No matter what you go through, do not give up. Keep fighting. You deserve to be blessed; you deserve love, peace, and joy. You deserve all the good things that come from the Lord, and He wants you to have it. Do not lose hope; keep the faith, keep pressing. Fight for your blessings.

Fight the good fight of the faith. Take hold of the eternal life to which you were called and about which you made the good confession in the presence of many witnesses. (1 Timothy 6:12).

Fighting for your blessings requires physical and spiritual strength to overcome your opponent. Which means you must prepare for the battle and arm yourself with the right tools so you can come out victorious.

Therefore take up the whole armor of God, that you may be able to withstand in the evil day, and having done all, to stand firm. (Ephesians 6:13).

Here are four strategies that will help when fighting for your blessings:

1. Use scriptures.

The Word of God is our defense against the enemy, the root of our strength, the life of our very existence, and the key to our peace of mind.

And, as shoes for your feet, having put on the readiness given by the gospel of peace. In all circumstances take up the shield of faith, with which you can extinguish all the flaming darts of the evil one; and take the helmet of salvation, and the sword of the Spirit, which is the word of God. (Ephesians 6:15-17).

2. Fast and pray.

There are certain results that only come through prayer and fasting. When you fast and pray, you lay down the flesh and take hold of your spirit man, which opens the gate to the spiritual realm where the presence of God dwells to:

- Pull down strongholds that have entangled our blessings.

- Overcome temptation.

- Put the devil in his corner.

3. Midnight prayer.

The midnight prayer is a bondage-breaking prayer, which will help you live a free and blessed life.

About midnight Paul and Silas were praying and singing hymns to God, and the prisoners were listening to them, and suddenly there was a great earthquake, so that the foundations of the prison were shaken. And immediately all the doors were opened, and everyone's bonds were unfastened. (Acts 16:25-26).

4. Be specific in what you are praying about.

There are times we are praying, and the only words we can utter is: "Lord, help me." Nothing is wrong with that, but it is better when you are specific. Also, when praying about your blessings, pray against the prince of Persia, who steals blessings. Ask God to send help to locate your blessings and let it be released into your life.

And he said to me, "O Daniel, man greatly loved, understand the words that I speak to you, and stand upright, for now I have been sent to you." And when he had spoken this word to me, I stood up trembling. Then he said to me, "Fear not, Daniel, for from the first day that you set your heart to understand and humbled yourself before your God, your words have been heard, and I have come because of your words. The prince of the kingdom of Persia withstood me twenty-one days, but Michael, one of the chief princes, came to help me, for I was left there with the kings of Persia." (Daniel 10:11-13).

Here are four good traits to acquire to obtain blessings:

1. Humility.

When I think of humility, I think of my mother. I have watched her go through so much over the years. The pain and hurt others have caused her were evident, and so was their wicked intentions that they carried out with joy. Yet, she never held it against them. She would be the first to help them without hesitation and even give of her last. One friend would say: "It looks like Jesus left one a Him slippers with her." I really believe when humility was being distributed, God gave her a double portion. She is such a humble soul with a pure heart. I know there is a great reward awaiting her when she gets to heaven.

The reward for humility and fear of the Lord is riches and honor and life. (Proverbs 22:4).

2. Faithfulness.

Aim to become faithful; faithful in works, faithful in deeds, and faithful in commitments. Be faithful in the little God has blessed you with, so He can entrust you with true riches.

If then you have not been faithful in the unrighteous wealth, who will entrust to you the true riches? (Luke 16:11).

3.   Persistence.

In whatever you seek to accomplish, when difficulties arise, stand your ground; hold firm to God in spite of your challenges, and you will receive your reward.

Whatever you do, work heartily, as for the Lord and not for men, knowing that from the Lord you will receive the inheritance as your reward. You are serving the Lord Christ. (Colossians 3:23-24).

4.   Visionary.

See beyond the barrier called poverty. Take hold of that dream, that vision which will cause you to prosper, succeed, and flourish.

Where there is no prophetic vision the people cast off restraint, but blessed is he who keeps the law. (Proverbs 29:18).

Use your God-given talent to get wealth. We all have a gift or a talent that God has blessed us with. Do not take it for granted; use it. You can access blessings by using your talent. Work at it, develop your talent; it can become your biggest source of blessings.

To one he gave five talents, to another two, to another one, to each according to his ability. Then he went away. (Matthew 25:15).

13
Greatest Blessings

The greatest blessing that is given to us is Jesus Christ. Through Him, all other blessings are accessible, as we accept the gift of salvation.

For God so loved the world, that he gave his only Son, that whoever believes in him should not perish but have eternal life. (John 3:16).

What is salvation? Salvation is being delivered or set free from sin, through the blood of Jesus Christ.

And there is salvation in no one else, for there is no other name under heaven given among men by which we must be saved. (Acts 4:12).

The only way in which we can access the gift of salvation is by confessing our sin and accepting Jesus Christ as Lord and Savior.

Because, if you confess with your mouth that Jesus is Lord and believe in your heart that God raised him from the dead, you will be saved. For with the heart one believes and is justified, and with the mouth one confesses and is saved. (Romans 10:9-10).

Prayer For Salvation

Dear Lord Jesus, I am a sinner. I believe You are the Son of God and that You died for my sins and arose from the dead. I accept You as my Lord and Savior, in Jesus name. Amen.

Prayer For Restoration

Mighty God, You said in Matthew 18:20 that where two are three are gathered touching anything concerning You, You are in the midst. So, Lord Jesus, I stand in agreement with Your child. Turn around his/her situation and let blessings overflow in his/her life. Show yourself strong, mighty God, and be glorified, in Jesus name. Amen.

Conclusion

I believe that from the moment of conception, God embedded in our DNA everything we need to accomplish His will for our lives. Similarly to how there are stages before you reach adulthood, there are stages and levels we must reach to awaken or reveal God's gifts, blessings, and purpose for our lives.

There are many detours and roadblocks that may occur, but by intentionally staying in God's presence, meditating on His Word, praying continually, and feeding our spirit man, we will become more aware of the enemy's (devil) devices and know how to fight, so even if we fall into a pothole, we will have the confidence that God will guide us safely through and lead us to His desired purpose for our lives.

Mother, you can make it! You have a powerful secret weapon: the holder of the universe, Jesus Christ. He has given you authority and power over everything under the heavens. Go forth, take charge, and live the life you so deserve.

About the Author

Franceta Lopez was born in Westmoreland, Jamaica. She relocated to Portmore, St. Catherine at three months old, where she still resides with her husband and their four boys. Franceta began writing at the age of twelve. She has written many articles and poems. She became fully committed to writing in 2015 when she lost her daughter, Gabrielle Lopez.

Franceta is a Christian empowerment life coach, motivational speaker, and the founder of *Mother You Can Make It*, a faith-based organization that is dedicated to elevating, building, and restoring mothers to the person God created them to be.

You can learn more about Franceta Lopez at:
https://www.facebook.com/motheryoucanmakeit/
https://www.motheryoucanmakeit.com